Lake Huron Rock Picker's Guide

Lake Huron
Rock Picker's Guide

Bruce Mueller
and
Kevin Gauthier

The University of Michigan Press
Ann Arbor
and
The Petoskey Publishing Company
Traverse City

Copyright © by the University of Michigan 2010
All rights reserved
Published in the United States of America by
The University of Michigan Press
and
The Petoskey Publishing Company
Manufactured in the United States of America
♾ Printed on acid-free paper

2013 2012 2011 2010   5 4 3 2 1

ISBN 978-0-472-03367-6   (paper : alk. paper)

No part of this publication may be reproduced, stored in a retrieval system, or transmitted in any form or by any means, electronic, mechanical, or otherwise, without written permission of the publishers.

This book is dedicated to the tens of thousands of men, women, and children whom it has been our pleasure to meet and get to know during our many years in business. Most of you came simply as people, though in our opinion all people are complex people. Some came as children, filled with curiosity and the desire to learn and to become, because childhood is about becoming. And some came dancing on that razor's edge, well described by Mary Shelley, which separates genius from insanity. It has been our privilege and pleasure to know all of you. We always look forward to seeing you again each year.

This book is dedicated to my brother
Scott Gauthier
Who has shown me how to live life with
a Big Heart-

-Kevin Gauthier

Contents

Introduction	9
Rock Picker's Guide to Lake Huron	11
Respect the Park's Rules	12
Lake Huron Geological History	13
A Trip around the Lake	21
Points # 1–3 from the Bridge to Alpena	21
Points # 4–7 from Alpena to Harrisville	25
Points # 8–9 Alabaster to Au Gres	34
Points # 10–11 Au Gres to Quanicassee	35
Points # 11–17 Quanicassee to Port Huron	35
Points # 18–21 Port Huron to Just South of Port Elgin	37
Points # 21–24 Port Elgin to Tobermory and Back to Craigleith	42
Points # 25–26 Craigleith to the Blue Mountains	44
Point # 27 Victoria Harbour to Exit 213	45
Point # 28 Exit 213 to Parry Sound	45
Point # 29 Parry Sound to Near Sudbury	46
Points # 30–31 South of Sudbury to Espanola	47
Points # 31–34 Espanola to Manitoulin Island	48
Trans-Canada Highway to Blind River	52
Points # 35–36 Blind River to Sault Ste. Marie	52
Points # 37–39 Sault Ste. Marie to Drummond Island	55
What Types of Rocks Are Found on Lake Huron?	61
Basalt	61
Chain coral	61
Chert	62
Cladopora	62
Crinoids	63
Dolomite	64
Favosite fossils (Charlevoix stone)	64
Feldspar	65

Gowganda tillite	65
Granite	66
Honeycomb coral	66
Horn corals	67
Jasper	68
Kettle stones	69
Petoskey stones	69
Pipe organ coral	69
Puddingstones	70
Quartz	71
Sandstone	71
Stromatoporoid	72
Syringopora	72
Trilobite	72
Unakite	73
The Passion of Rock Collecting	74

Color photographs *following page* 48

Introduction

Pavé jewelry is covered with gems. Lake Huron is pavéd with gemlike islands. Georgian Bay alone is said to have 30,000 islands. We have not counted every one and, because we consider it statistically improbable that anything natural would add up to such a nice round number, suspect that 30,000 islands is simply a rough estimate of a nearly uncountable number of islands. In addition, the region is home to many more islands in Potagannissing Bay, the Saint Marys River, and the Les Cheneaux Islands grouping. Some of the larger islands such as Bois Blanc Island, Drummond Island, Sugar Island, and Manitoulin Island can be reached by bridge or ferry or both, and some are surrounded by satellite islands that hover near like groupies around a rock star band. Manitoulin Island, the world's largest island in a freshwater lake, has its own interior lake—and that lake has its own island. By the time all of Lake Huron's shoreline mileage is added up, including that of its islands, bays, and peninsulas, you will have, we believe, the longest shoreline of any freshwater lake on earth.

On that shoreline, the bedrock ranges from sedimentary to igneous to metamorphic, with the igneous rock ranging from intrusive to extrusive. Above the bedrock is glacial debris brought in from as far away as the Arctic Coast of Canada, from the bottom of Hudson Bay (and probably James Bay), and from the floors of what are now lakes, forests, and muskeg. Stirred into this wild mix of boulders, cobbles, and pebbles from every existing rock type, there may be samples scraped from the bedrock on the eastern shore of the Hudson Bay—at 4.28 billion years of age, this is the oldest rock yet found on earth. Finally, there may be samples of stones that are as yet unknown and unnamed. We think we've found a few of these ourselves. They make you scratch your head, stroke your beard (whether you have one or not), and wonder: what is this, and what coded message does it bear from an unimaginably distant past?

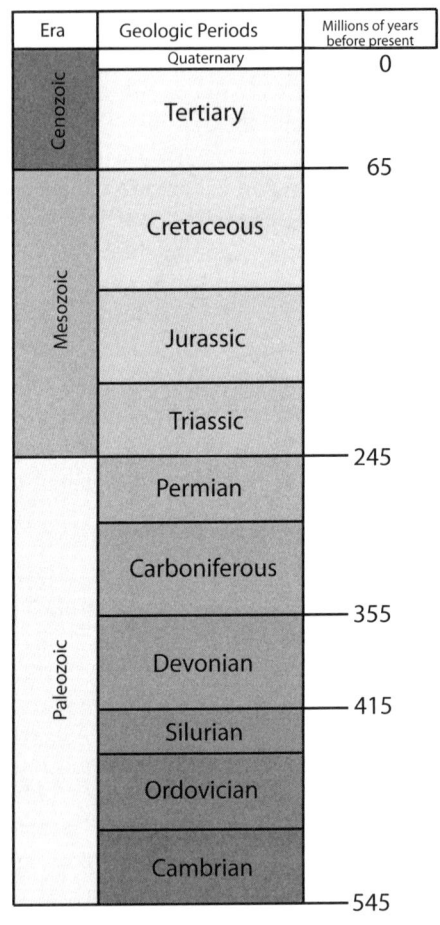

Era	Geologic Periods	Millions of years before present
Cenozoic	Quaternary	0
Cenozoic	Tertiary	
		65
Mesozoic	Cretaceous	
Mesozoic	Jurassic	
Mesozoic	Triassic	
		245
Paleozoic	Permian	
Paleozoic	Carboniferous	
		355
Paleozoic	Devonian	
		415
Paleozoic	Silurian	
Paleozoic	Ordovician	
Paleozoic	Cambrian	
		545

Fig. 1. The geologic time line

Rock Picker's Guide to Lake Huron

Stones on Lake Huron beaches and the fossils and minerals they contain pose questions for those who find them. It is those questions this book was written to answer:

What is it?
Where is it from?
How did it get here?
How old is it?
What does it say about the past?

Mohs Scale of Hardness		Hardness of Common Objects	
Diamond	10		
Corundum (ruby, sapphire)	9	8.5	wet/dry silicon carbide and sandpaper
Topaz	8		
Quartz	7		
Feldspar	6	6.5	hardened steel (file)
Apatite	5	5.5	knife blade or glass
Flourite	4		
Calcite	3	3	copper (penny dated 1980 or earlier)
Gypsum	2	2.5	fingernail
Talc	1		

You can test the hardness of rocks by using common objects to do a scratch test. If the object scratches the rock, the rock is softer than the object. If the object leaves a streak on the rock, the rock is harder than the object. Example: Beach garnet (Canadian Shield rock) is a hardness of 6.5–7; a copper penny (hardness of 3) would leave a streak. Likewise most fossils like Petoskey stones (Devonian rock) can be scratched by a knife blade.

Respect the Park's Rules

Keep in mind that you are sharing and using the same beaches with many other people. The parks and places mentioned in this book should be treated with respect, following their rules and regulations. The rules for collecting vary from state to state and from park to park. There are national parks, state parks, county parks, township parks, city parks, and there is private property. It's best to check in advance before collecting. In general the more important the park, national or state, the less likely collecting will be allowed. Some park officials are more lenient than others. Where collecting is permitted, take only a few specimens, which the waves will replenish, and leave only footprints behind.

For listing of parks see the following Web sites:

www.michigandnr.com
www.pc.gc.ca

Lake Huron Geological History

Although beach composition varies greatly, about half of the stones on an average shoreline are local bedrock. All other rocks, except those trucked in for erosion control, have been brought in by glacial transport from one of two vast and divergent rock systems: the Michigan Basin System and the Canadian Shield System.

The Canadian Shield covers 2 million square miles and is composed primarily of granite that has melted its way up from below to form a wildly diverse landscape of rock. Largely assembled from miscellaneous bits and pieces brought in from elsewhere, this rock was scraped off as the seafloor was subducted below the Shield. A similar process is currently occurring in portions of California west of the San Andreas Fault and the Baja Peninsula. This area is moving with the Pacific seafloor plate toward the Alaskan Peninsula at a rate of 20 feet per hundred years. One day in the near future (as geologic time goes), they will be part of Alaska.

To further complicate the picture, much of the Canadian Shield has been folded to form mountain ranges, now largely eroded down to their metamorphosed roots. Canadian Shield rocks are almost always harder than a knife blade, and they are old—up to 4.28 billion years old—with granite being relatively younger and the basalts and metamorphic rock generally older.

In contrast, Michigan Basin rock is young, sedimentary, and almost always softer than a knife blade. The basin was formed during the earth's early history when an asteroid impact or down-warping caused by the rising of a distant mountain range created a basin in the earth's surface. Once created, the Basin began to fill with sediment brought in by rivers and marine invasions. The Basin filled with sediment from its outer edge inward. Seen from above with all soil and glacial debris removed, these layers form a targetlike pattern with the bull's eye, the youngest rock in the system, located at Midland, Michigan. Seen from below Midland in cross-section, the oldest layers are on the bottom with each overlying layer younger.

The outer edge of the Michigan Basin is marked by the Niagaran Escarpment (so-called because Niagara Falls flows over its edge along an entrance way to the Michigan Basin). Much of the Niagaran Escarpment can be seen on any map of the Great Lakes. The Escarpment was formed during the Silurian period when seawater moved across what is now New York State, along what is now the St. Lawrence River Valley, and into the Basin. This water flowed in just fast enough to replace evaporation, leading

Michigan Basin

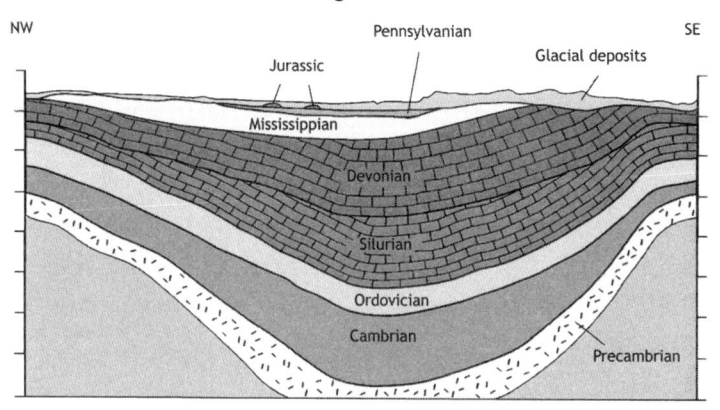

Fig. 2. Hypothetical geological cross-section through the Michigan Basin. Section is idealized along a line from southeastern (on the right) to the northeastern (on the left) part of southern peninsula of Michigan. (Adapted from the Michigan Department of Natural Resources and Environment, Office of Geological Survey, Bulletin 06 "Mineralogy of Michigan Revised," 2004.)

it to grow saltier as time went on. As water becomes more saline, its least soluble elements start being deposited. In this case, limestone, composed primarily of shell fragments from marine organisms as well as from evaporation, was deposited around the Basin's edges and across its floor. As the water continued to increase in salinity, magnesium replaced some of the calcium in the limestone to create a hard, resistant layer of dolomite (a calcium magnesium carbonate). This conversion to dolomite caused the rock to lose volume and become harder, more acid resistant, and more porous. The process also typically degraded any fossils present.

Marking the outer edge of the Michigan Basin, the Niagaran Escarpment encloses Michigan's Lower Peninsula, Lake Michigan with the exception of Green Bay, Lake Huron with the exception of Georgian Bay, the eastern portion of Michigan's Upper Peninsula, eastern Wisconsin, the northeast corner of Illinois, northern Indiana, northern Ohio, the western half of Lake Erie (where it has no surface expression), and southwestern Ontario. Physical expressions of the Escarpment can be seen throughout the region, starting with the Bruce Peninsula, which separates Lake Huron from Georgian Bay. Following the curve made by the Bruce Peninsula leads to a string of islands, among them Manitoulin Island and Drummond Island. Following the same curve across the Lower Peninsula leads to the Garden Peninsula and eventually to another string of islands and Wisconsin's Dorr County Peninsula. From here, the Escarpment forms the western edge of Lake Michigan through Chicago. Further evidence of the Escarpment can be found near Thornton, Illinois, a suburb of Chicago, where one of the world's largest quarries extracts material from what was once a reef on the Escarpment. The dolomite layer then passes through Indiana and Ohio and back to the Bruce Peninsula.

Just inside the Niagaran Escarpment are layers of younger, softer rock that were formed as the seawater in the Basin continued to grow saltier and deposited additional minerals. Among these was alabaster, today mined at Alabaster, Michigan, a major producer of the gypsum used in the manufacture of wallboard. (Note that other alabaster formerly mined below Grand Rapids is of a younger age.) Additionally, a layer of various salts accumulated, ranging from only about 500 feet thick around the Basin's edges to, with minor interruptions, around 2,000 feet thick near its center at Midland, Michigan. This layer contains table salt, bromine, calcium chloride, iodine, and other valuable chemicals that can be pumped from the ground as brine. It is for this reason that Dow Chemical started in Midland, where these salts are concentrated.

These soft layers along with a layer of soft shale known as the Antrim Shale were cut downward by the Wisconsin glacier to create Lakes Michigan and Huron, with the Niagaran Escarpment serving as the outer edge of each. In a very real sense these two lakes are mirror images. Lake Michigan lies along the west side of the basin and bows outward toward the west following the curve of the basin; Lake Huron lies along the east side of the basin and bows outward toward the east following the curve of the basin. Walk south from the Big Mac Bridge on either lake's shore, and you will encounter nearly the same rock layers in the same order.

1. Devonian
2. Antrim Shale Devonian and Mississippian
3. Mississippian
4. Pennsylvanian
5. Jurassic

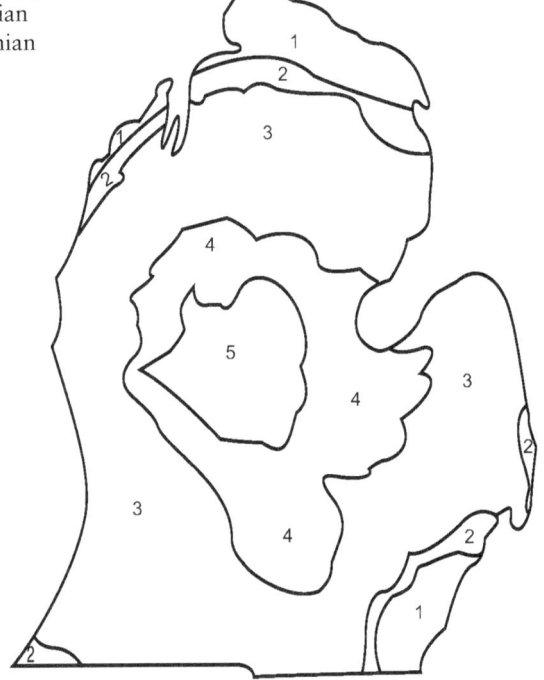

Fig. 3. Note the targetlike pattern of sedimentary layers deposited during five geological periods in the Lower Peninsula of Michigan, which is the basin's center.

Lake Huron Rock Picker's Guide 19

One way to determine the age of bedrock within the Michigan Basin is by its position (see fig. 3). The closer the bedrock is to Midland, the younger it is. However, rock is sometimes transported from one place to another, unless it is bedrock. Its location is not always an appropriate way to determine age. Because rock in the Michigan Basin is sedimentary, there is often another way to easily determine its age: fossils within the rock. When shallow inland seas form as they did in the Michigan Basin, similar seas form in other locations worldwide. These seas absorbed warmth from the sun to create a warm stable climate, hospitable to whatever organisms were living in the sea at the time. When these seas began to withdraw, the climate became less stable. Marine organisms can be pushed to extinction by a temperature change of as little as 3 degrees, and so many organisms became extinct.

Out at sea, new organisms evolved. In the ocean, the fossil record of this constant evolution was erased as the seafloor vanished beneath the continents due to subduction—this was not the case, however, in shallow inland seas like the ones that covered Michigan. When the water returned to these seas, a vast array of newly evolved organisms came with it. In turn, these organisms eventually went extinct, some leaving records of themselves in the form of fossils, and were then replaced by still newer species. As the process continued, layers of fossils were laid down, like isolated scenes from a play spanning over 600 million years. Certain organisms will appear in one scene but be absent from the preceding and succeeding scenes. By getting to know a few of these players and at what point they entered the drama, we can immediately recognize the age of the bedrock in which they appear, regardless of whether or not it has been glacially transported. For example, halysites (well known as chain coral to any who have walked the beaches of Lake Michigan or Huron) inhabited the Niagaran Escarpment from the late Ordovician to the Middle Silurian. Because of this, we know rocks containing fossilized halysites must have been formed during those periods—that is, 461 million to 416 million years ago.

Fossils are the key to the age of sedimentary rocks. The book *Index Fossils of North America,* by Harvey W. Shimer and Robert Rakes Shrock, lists a tremendous number of fossils (maybe 8,000) and the time periods during which they lived. Though now out of print, the book can be found in many large libraries. Another source for information on fossils is *Geology of Michigan,* by John A. Dorr, Jr., and Donald F. Eschman (ISBN 978-0-472-08280-3).

A Trip around the Lake

Anything east of the Mackinac Bridge might be considered Lake Huron, so the Big Mac is a logical place to start a trip around the lake. Across the bridge lies the Niagaran Escarpment. Below the bridge are seven miles of water, where the extremely soluble Silurian anhydrite and salt layers are close to the surface. A major inactive fault runs along the St. Lawrence River and passes under the bridge. In the past, when sea level was low, water draining out along the fault dissolved the layers of anhydrite and salt, undermining the overlying rock, causing collapse and shattering of the sediments above. Such collapses occurred repeatedly for hundreds of millions of years. The result: the Straits of Mackinac. Near the Straits you will see shattered rock, some of it reduced to the size of gravel, on either side of the bridge, along the Straits, and on Mackinac Island.

Points # 1–3 from the Bridge to Alpena

Devonian Bedrock, Limestone, and Dolomite

To the southeast of Cheboygan lies Black Lake. Here and along rivers in this area, *Hexagonaria* fossils can be found. These colonial corals, commonly called Petoskey stones, can

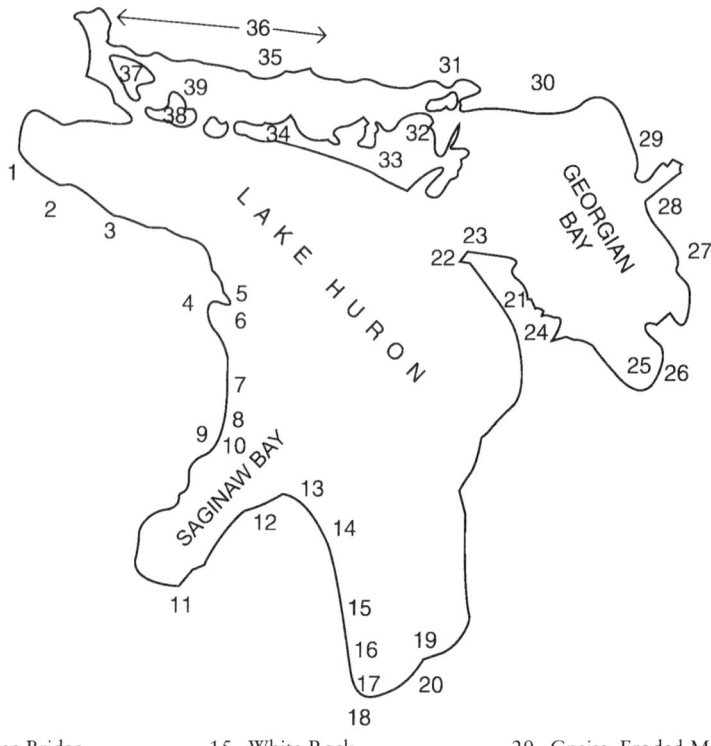

1. Big Mac Bridge
2. Black Lake
3. Hammond
4. Alpena
5. Partridge Point
6. Sulfur Island
7. Sturgeon Point
8. Alabaster
9. Whitestone Point
10. Charity Island
11. Quanicassee
12. Port Crescent State Park
13. Grindstone City
14. Pointe Aux Barques Lighthouse
15. White Rock
16. Tierney Harbor Park
17. Fort Gratiot
18. Port Huron and Sarnia
19. Kettle or Concretion Park
20. Arkona
21. Ferndale
22. Tobermory
23. Flowerpot Island
24. Upper Ordovician Rock
25. Craigleith
26. Blue Mountain and Caves
27. Gneiss, Eroded Mountain Roots
28. Former Volcanic Islands
29. Gneiss, Eroded Mountain Roots
30. Sedimentary Rock
31. La Cloche Mountains
32. Sheguiandah
33. Manitoulin Island
34. Meldrum Bay or Manitoulin Quarry
35. Metamorphic or Igneous Rock
36. Gowganda Tillite, Puddingstone, and Gordon Lake
37. St. Joseph Island
38. Drummond Island
39. Fossil Ledges

Fig. 4. Location points for a trip around the lake

weigh up to twenty pounds or more. The skeletons of these corals have filled with calcite from the outside, a process that closed off the corals' porous interiors. Usually only a thin shell can be polished on the exterior, but this shell can be very beautiful. See figure 4 for locations.

Fossilized corals from the Niagaran Escarpment and upper Lower Peninsula have been glacially transported to the Lake Huron shoreline, though more commonly to the northern parts of the lake where the source is closer. As previously mentioned, the conversion of limestone to dolomite that occurred where these corals originated seriously degraded fossils contained within the rock, but halysites (often called chain coral) and syringopora from the escarpment are notable exceptions. By some process, these two corals, along with some horn corals, were replaced with quartz before dolomitization could take place, leaving their extraordinarily intricate and fragile structures intact.

It's possible to extract these fossils from dolomite. Dolomite is slowly soluble in muriatic acid, which is available at any hardware store. By sanding dolomite fossils flat on the bottom and spraying this surface with lacquer to prevent solution, you can create a base for support. Next, immerse the fossil in water, and add acid from time to time. Always use care when using acid: work outdoors and neutralize remaining acid with limestone or crushed marble (which are available as landscaping supplies). Do NOT pour the acid down the drain.

It may take several days or more for solution of the dolomite. Once solution has occurred, remove the fossil carefully as it will be fragile until dry. The result will be a fossil such as can seldom be collected anywhere. Syringopora has cross members to hold its columns together and can, therefore, be removed entirely from its stony tomb. Sometimes horn corals can be exposed attached to the interiors of these tiny coral reefs.

US 23 from Nine Mile Point to Hammond runs close to the lake. Many beaches here are pure sand, but at Huron Shores Park and other beaches along the way to Hammond Bay State Park a variety of interesting specimens can be collected, including stromatoporoids, favosites and corals of several other species, brachiopods, cladopora, basalt, chert, puddingstone, and Gowganda tillite. Walk ten paces on one of these beaches, and you will find something astonishing. At Huron Shores in particular there is an unusual amount of quartzite, most likely brought down from the Gordon Lake sediments to the north in Canada; some of it is banded and of unusual color and beauty.

Washed by muriatic acid, this chain coral's rock has been removed leaving a pristine coral. See the color photo section to see what these fossils look like on the beach encased in stone.

Points # 4–7 from Alpena to Harrisville

Devonian Shale and Limestone

Alpena is an exceptional place for fossil collecting. Many of the area's best fossil sites are described in *The Complete Guide to Michigan Fossils*, by Joseph Kchodl (ISBN 978-0-472 03149-8), which we recommend to anyone interested in collecting here.

Muriatic acid bath exposes the true nature of the syringopora

The shale here is known as the Antrim Shale because it is exposed in Antrim County near Norwood, Michigan. Ranging in age from Devonian to Mississippian, the shale on rare occasions contains armor-plated Devonian fish. Large round stones called concretions (or kettle stones) that have grown within the shale as it was compressed can also be found here. Until 1994, the Antrim Shale was excavated at the Paxton Quarry near Alpena, Michigan, one of the few places where these concretions sometimes contain rare fossils of land plants from the late Devonian, the time of the first forests. The Jesse Besser Museum (phone: 989 356-2202) in Alpena displays some of the finest examples of these fossils.

In Alpena at the Lafarge Quarry (phone: 989-354-4171), limestone is quarried and mixed with slag from the Chicago area rather than the shale formerly used to manufacture concrete. Quarries where stone is blasted and loose blocks are left hanging can be dangerous, and their owners rarely conduct tours because of insurance considerations. On occasion, however, these quarries dump an amount of quarry rock in flat, level areas for the public to examine—sometimes very nice trilobites can be found here. If you would like to visit a quarry, it is advisable to call well in advance and make an appointment; they may let you in—the key word being *may*. If you do visit a quarry, always stay out of situations that appear unsafe. If you do not and are injured, blame no one but yourself.

One of the best known collecting sites in the Alpena area is Partridge Point—if you go, a hammer for splitting limestone layers will be helpful. Four miles south of Alpena on US 23, turn east on Partridge Point Rd S and head toward the lake. After driving 1.6 miles, you will see a two-track road to the right that, while probably drivable, may be more safely walked. A short walk up this road will reveal Devonian limestone bedrock that contains several types of trilobites, many brachiopods, very large horn corals, large favosites, and many other invertebrate fossils. Walking east along the shoreline, with luck you may find petrified wood toward and beyond the end of the point. This is petrified fern tree wood, identifiable by bark impressions on its exterior and notably missing the growth lines and radials found in other petrified woods. Much of the petrified wood that can be collected here is composed of opaque, amorphous quartz that is black in color, probably due to carbon in the tree trunk. Sigillaria, lepidodendron, and calamites were some of the common and very large fern trees, and they can be recognized by their bark.

In the coal-age swamps of the late Devonian, the Mississippian, and the Pennsylvanian, gelatin-like colonies of bacteria accumulated clay, calcium carbonate, and iron carbonate. When these colonies died, they would be buried and begin to dry. As this occurred, the soft stony material would crack and eventually be filled with white calcite and sometimes other minerals such as quartz, galena, and sphalerite. These can be found on Sulfur Island just offshore from Partridge Point. They are similar to the lightning stones found at South Haven, Michigan as discussed in the *Lake Michigan Rock Picker's Guide* (ISBN 978-0-472-03150-4).

> STURGEON POINT
> LIGHTHOUSE
> ALCONA HISTORICAL SOCIET
> IN COOPERATION WITH
> MICHIGAN DEPARTMENT OF
> NATURAL RESOURCES
> PARKS AND RECREATION DIVISION

From the top of Sturgeon Point Lighthouse, an exceptional pop-up can be seen. The Wisconsin glacier (which lasted from about 100,000 to 10,000 years ago) was so heavy that it caused the land to subside in a downward arc. When the glacier melted, the land began to rebound, and there was compression between one side of the arc and the other. The result: a fracture where one side of the land rose more than the other. This fracture has brought granite to the surface, resulting in the creation of a point that runs a half mile or more offshore, including an underwater segment. Granite boulders the size of houses can be seen underwater here. Further evidence of the underwater

Looking out Sturgeon Point Lighthouse onto the granite
that runs a half mile into Lake Huron

ridge is the wave action: waves slow down and are bent as they enter shallow water, breaking on both sides of this point and depositing gravel that is up to and beyond cobble sized. This gravel is Canadian Shield material, composed especially of puddingstone and Gowganda tillite as well as bedrock fossils, including trilobites and other marine invertebrates.

Looking back at Sturgeon Point Lighthouse

Lighthouse interior

Alcona Historical Society has replicated the Sturgeon Bay Lighthouse's original living quarters, and tours are available for a small fee. The surrounding area, filled with a lot of rocks, great views, and plenty to take in, is definitely worth spending an afternoon exploring.

"Live for the now, for each day those moments add up to who you are."

—Debra J. Engar

Why are porous/soft Petoskey stones found in Alpena?

When people tell us they know where hundreds of pounds of Petoskey stones can be found, our first question is usually, "Are they from the east side of Michigan?" The reason we ask this is that most Petoskey stones found east of I-75 are porous and what many consider low grade. Large quarries in and around Alpena have produced numerous Petoskey stones and on occasion just "dump" this material into an area deemed no-man's-land—these stones often are porous and do not take a high polish.

We believe that the reason for the difference between Petoskey stones on the east and west sides of the state can be traced back 350 million years. The coral that became Petoskey stones originally grew in a shallow inland sea that covered northern Michigan. We think that chemical and physical conditions varied from one side of this sea to the other. The shale to the west came in as mud from a high area in Wisconsin known as the Wisconsin Arch. The shale on the east came in from the Appalachians when they first began to rise in the east. The water to the west is believed to have been oxygen deficient, preventing decomposition.

Points # 8–9 Alabaster to Au Gres

Alabaster and Chert

At Alabaster, Michigan, there is, as the city's name suggests, alabaster. Differing from gypsum only in water content, alabaster is white with orange patches and black stringers. Alabaster is primarily used in building materials like plaster of paris and wallboard, but, being soft and easily carved, it is also often used to make lamp bases and decorative utilitarian objects. There are alabaster quarries (both abandoned and operating) everywhere, including a few on Twining and Bessinger roads. However, access to these quarries is typically somewhere between difficult and impossible.

Two very nice gentlemen run a string of cabins near Au Gres at Whitestone Point (mailing address: 5883 S. Lake Lane Drive, Au Gres, Michigan 48703; toll free phone: 866 820-6414). Large chert nodules are abundant on the Point as well as just offshore on Charity Island. These are must visit locations for flint knappers—Native Americans are said to have collected material for arrowheads here. Chert can be distinguished from flint by its primarily light coloration and its occurrence in nodules; flint is dark colored and occurs in layers. Banded or patterned chert often makes good cabochons.

Points # 10–11 Au Gres to Quanicassee

Pennsylvanian Rock

Long ago there were coal mines between Au Gres and Quanicassee, but their waste piles have long since grassed over. Throughout this interior section of Saginaw Bay, any sandy beaches are typically lacking rock and tend to belong to private homeowners. In the places without houses, the shoreline is usually marshy with grass taller than your head. Again, there are few rocks.

Points # 11–17 Quanicassee to Port Huron

Mississippian Siltstone and Sandstone

Route 25 leads to the northernmost of the two Port Crescent State Parks and from there to Grindstone Point and Grindstone City. These places took their names from the great circular wheels of siltstone cut from the area's bedrock and used for sharpening metal tools. Some grindstones were six feet in diameter and had a central hole about the size of a four-by-four. Grindstones were manufactured here from bedrock between 1836 and 1929, when carborundum, an inferior but cheaper substitute, came into use.

Large grinding stone at Grindstone City

A harbor was created at Grindstone City by two piers, constructed of large boulders of Canadian Shield rock, Gowganda tillite, basalt, and gabbro (basalt that cooled slowly enough to be coarsely granular). Similar boulders, probably from a nearby gravel pit, have been dumped throughout the area in order to prevent shoreline erosion.

A Huron County park at Pointe Aux Barques Lighthouse is to the southeast of Grindstone City, and walking along the shore here near the lighthouse, enormous slabs of siltstone can be seen lying on the bottom of the bay. A boat trip reveals that these awesome slabs continue offshore as well.

To the south at White Rock, there is, appropriately enough, a white rock half a mile offshore. Twelve feet by twelve feet square, the rock rises from the floor of the lake to stand four feet above the water. Said to have been struck by lightning many times, it is almost certainly a great piece from the Niagaran Escarpment transported here by the Wisconsin glacier. The rock once stood as a boundary line separating settlers and Native Americans and was later used for target practice by the air force during World War Two.

Still farther south at Tierney Harbor Park near Lexington, there is sand and many small pebbles of brown chert, some of which contain invertebrate fossils such as brachiopods. At Fort Gratiot there is large glacial gravel, including Petoskey stones, puddingstones, Gowganda tillite, brachiopods, corals of various types, and the usual marine invertebrate fossils. The bedrock is shale reduced to mud by water saturation.

Points # 18–21 Port Huron to Just South of Port Elgin

Devonian Limestone and Shale

At Kettle Point, Ontario, locally called Concretion Point, there is a park where concretions in the Antrim Shale lie exposed both on shore and out in the lake. The shale here

A kettle stone at Kettle Point

(the same as in Norwood and Alpena, Michigan) came from the newly risen Appalachians to the east; the shale at Norwood came from a high area called the Wisconsin Arch. It would take an 800-pound gorilla to pick up one of these stones. Even if you were that strong, please remember that this is a park—no collecting. Outside of the park, a little to the north or south, you should be able to find paper-thin layers of Kettle Point Shale. A 10-power lens or a binocular microscope will reveal fossils replaced by pyrite in this rock. These fossils include radiolaria (one-celled organisms that build amazingly geometric shells); fragments of sponges called spicules; and conodonts, tiny teeth of unknown origin, perhaps from minnows or worms. Carbonized and silicified wood is also present, and pyrite representing fossil algae is common.

Not far from Kettle Point, near Cleveland, Ohio, rock known locally as the Cleveland Shale can be found. Very likely an extension of the Antrim Shale, the Cleveland Shale is notable for producing a fossilized skull of an armor-plated fish named *Dunkleosteus terrelli*, sometimes referred to as an arthrodire shark. One of the finest of these huge fossils is currently housed in the Cleveland Museum of Natural History (phone: 216 231-4600). It is one of the best fossils of any kind ever found, and probably the greatest example of a Devonian fossil fish.

Fossils such as these take years to properly remove and prepare. Because of this, amateur paleontologists are ethically (and, in fact, legally) obligated to leave the investigation of these fossils to experts. Please do not take a sledge hammer to hundreds of concretions in hopes of finding an armor-plated fish -you'll not find one. Even if you were to, lacking proper training and experience, you'll almost certainly damage (or more probably destroy) invaluable information about the earth's past.

Route 79 near Arkona leads to Rock Glen Conservation Area and a waterfall on the Ausable River. As with the Niagara River at Niagara Falls, the Ausable

Cast of *Dunkleosteus terrelli* from the Devonian period at Augustana College. (Picture courtesy of William R. Hammer, Professor of Geology.)

has cut through a limestone caprock to expose and undercut a thick bed of Devonian Shale, bluish in color. The shale here is notable for containing a particular brachiopod named mucrospirifer, distinguished by wide winglike extensions on either side of its body. This fossil from the Middle Devonian often weathers out of the shale intact and is known locally as a butterfly stone. In places where the limestone caprock has collapsed into the canyon due to undercutting by the waterfall, trilobites and complete crinoids can occasionally be found,

Tire tracks on the sandy beach—no rocks

but will require quite a bit of looking. Phacops, greenops, and other trilobites can be found here, but good specimens are uncommon.

The beaches from Kettle Point to the Bruce Peninsula are composed of tiny fragments of shale, sand, and little else. If you were to plow a furrow along this beach (which, strangely enough, has actually been done here to keep the waves off the upper beach) you would likely find a pebble only every hundred feet or so. The beach is almost as smooth and solid as a blacktop highway, creating what looks like the world's longest drag strip—a hundred or so miles of sand interrupted here and there by streams. There are cars and tire tracks all over the beach.

Points # 21–24 Port Elgin to Tobermory and Back to Craigleith

Silurian Dolomite and Ordovician Shale

Here you will be crossing layers of limestone, dolomite, shale, sandstone, gypsum, and salt. Only the hardest of these, the dolomite of the Niagaran escarpment, has any real surface expression. Because the dolomite here tilts downward toward the center of the Michigan Basin, Georgian Bay is lined with high cliffs. This, combined with the bay's deep water, made diving and cliff jumping popular here, but laws were passed prohibiting these activities after a number of deaths. There are plenty of fossils in the dolomite, but they're mostly of poor quality. In places on Highway 6 (especially seven miles south of Ferndale), there are concretions largely composed of sphalerite, an ore of zinc. These are darker (bluish gray) than the surrounding rock. Elsewhere there are fossils replaced by sphalerite as well as near-gem-grade sphalerite in cavitiles. Along this shoreline there is a cave

Trilobite tail section fossil. (Courtesy of Craigleith Provincial Park, NO COLLECTING HERE.)

with an internal lagoon into which one can dive and swim out into Georgian Bay.

Beyond Tobermory there is an underwater shipwreck park where many sunken vessels may be viewed through glass-bottomed boats. Nearby Flowerpot Island has an enormous pot-shaped stone erosional remnant. From Tobermory, a ferry (for reservations, phone: 800 265-3183) connects to the next segment of the Niagaran Escarpment, Manitoulin Island. Along the northern base of the Bruce Peninsula, from Cape Commodore to Balmy Beach on Route 1, the rock is Upper Ordovician in age and contains many brachiopods, halysites, and large favosites coral colonies.

Points # 25-26 Craigleith to the Blue Mountains

Shale and Limestone

On Route 26 near Craigleith, there is a provincial park where camping facilities are available. Please remember this park is dedicated to preserving fossils, so collecting is not allowed here; the park is very serious about this. The beach contains shale and accompanying limestone that holds many fossil trilobites. Millions of years ago, trilobites shed their shells much as crayfish do today. Most of these shells broke apart when shed—fossilized tail sections are most frequently found. Isotelus, a particular kind of trilobite, is particularly common in this area. Some of the better specimens found here can be seen in the park office.

Just behind the park is Blue Mountain, the remnants of a mountainlike reef that once rose above the dolomite of the Niagaran Escarpment. In its day, this reef may have extended above the water's surface to form an island much like some modern reefs do today. The height of Blue

Mountain indicates just how deep the water was that once stood across this area 425 million years or more ago. Toward the top of Blue Mountain, there are a series of tall, wide, mostly shallow caves that are open to the public for an entry fee (for more information, call: 705 446-0256). Once occupied by Huron and Petun Indians, these caves are of varying sizes—one is only about fourteen inches high and known as Fat Man's Misery. Within the caves, the fossilized organisms that constructed the reefs are visible.

Point # 27 Victoria Harbour to Exit 213

Canadian Shield, Primarily Gneiss

These rocks vary greatly from mile to mile and represent the eroded roots of an ancient mountain range that at one time may have been broader and higher than the Himalayas. These rocks are 0.9 to 1.6 billion years old.

Point # 28 Exit 213 to Parry Sound

Dark Volcanic Rock Related to Basalt and Gabbro

At about 1.5 billion years old, the rock in this area is believed to have been part of a chain of ancient volcanoes that formed a thousand miles away or more. These volcanoes were rafted along by the seafloor and eventually scraped off as the plate subducted below the Canadian Shield, building the Shield up.

Point # 29 Parry Sound to Near Sudbury

Canadian Shield, Primarily Gneiss

The roots of the same mountain range extending from Victoria Harbour to Exit 213 can be seen here. The rocks in this area are gneiss and related metamorphosed sedimentary rock as well as unusual sandstones, all 0.9 to 1.6 billion years old. Particularly abundant here is phyllite, a sparkly, reflective, muscovite mica-filled metamorphic rock that formed when slate was compressed—further compression would result in the rock's metamorphosis into gneiss. Phyllite is attractive and usually splits into thin, flat sheets, making it popular for stepping stones and rock gardens.

At the time of research, this portion of the Canadian highway between Parry Sound and near Sudbury was under miles of construction—and presumably will be for some time. Construction crews worked to level the terrain to make building a road possible. Miles of freshly blasted rock were heaped into enormous piles, and hundreds of thousands of tons of granite were used to fill in mountain valleys—an amazing sight to see. At the proper turnouts, the construction allowed for some easy collection of striped garden rocks.

Points # 30–31 South of Sudbury to Espanola

Sedimentary Rock, Unusual Sandstone, Conglomerate Limestone, and Dolomite

The rocks here are sedimentary with occasional vertical (dikes) and horizontal (sills) intrusions by igneous rock, mostly dark basalt. The rock is around 2.2 billion years old. The presence of fossils is unlikely, but occasionally stromatoporoids—ancient laminated layers created by primitive algae—can be found.

Points # 31–34 Espanola to Manitoulin Island

Sedimentary Rock, Metamorphosed Sediments, and Intrusive Rock

The drive from Espanola to Whitefish Falls features incredibly beautiful scenery. A mountain range formed here 1.7 billion years ago, and its remains make up the La Cloche Mountains just north of Manitoulin Island. These mountains are partially composed of nearly pure white quartz sand that has been crushed together until its grains merged into quartzite. This quartzite tends to be tilted up on edge in the La Cloche Mountains. Quartzite has long been quarried in the area and to some degree still is today. Near Sheguiandah, Native Americans used the quartzite to make arrowheads and other artifacts about 9,500 years ago—modern flint knappers may find it useful as well. Similar quartzite can be found to the south along Lake Huron beaches in Michigan, and its origin is probably the La Cloche Mountains.

Basalt boulder

Basalt with quartz

Chain coral after acid wash

Chain coral

Chain coral jewelry

Chert

Cladopora, polished and natural

Crinoid top

Crinoid stem

Crinoid disks

Dolomite with holes

Water on dolomite

Dolomite in fifteen feet of water (note how blue the water appears)

Favosite fossil jewelry

Favosite fossils

Pieces of granite

Feldspar (note the sheen)

Gowganda tillite, found on the beach

Gowganda tillite, sliced

Horn coral specimens

Large horn coral

Honeycomb coral, calcified

Honeycomb coral, quartz-replaced

Red jasper

Kettle stone in shale

Kettle stone split open

Petoskey stones

Pipe organ coral head

Pipe organ coral

Petoskey stone jewelry

The Petoskey stone

Large puddingstone

Puddingstone expert Michael Seaman

Rare example of green quartz in puddingstone

Quartz

Sandstone

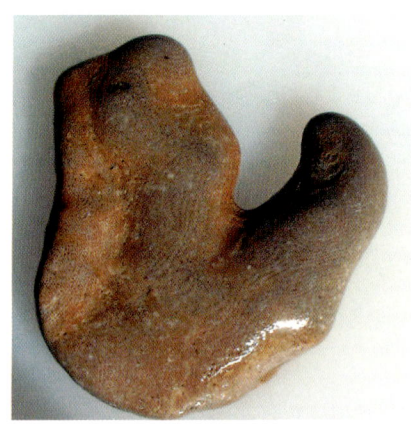

Stromatoporoid (petrified sponge)

Stromatoporoid and favosite

Syringopora jewelry

Syringopora, acid washed

Trilobite found at Craigleith

Trilobite

Unakite

Unakite lighthouse

Lake Huron Rock Picker's Guide 49

Goat Island lies on the route to Manitoulin Island. Tarps cover portions of Goat Island where the soil has been contaminated. A rail line once ran through the area, tearing up much of the bedrock. Many fossils, including trilobites, crinoids, and stromatoporoids—some in excellent condition—can be found here. The favosites corals are often hollow and filled with orange calcite.

On Manitoulin Island near Mississagi Lighthouse is one of Canada's largest quarries. In this quarry, an extraordinarily rare fossil known as a eurypterid or sea scorpion

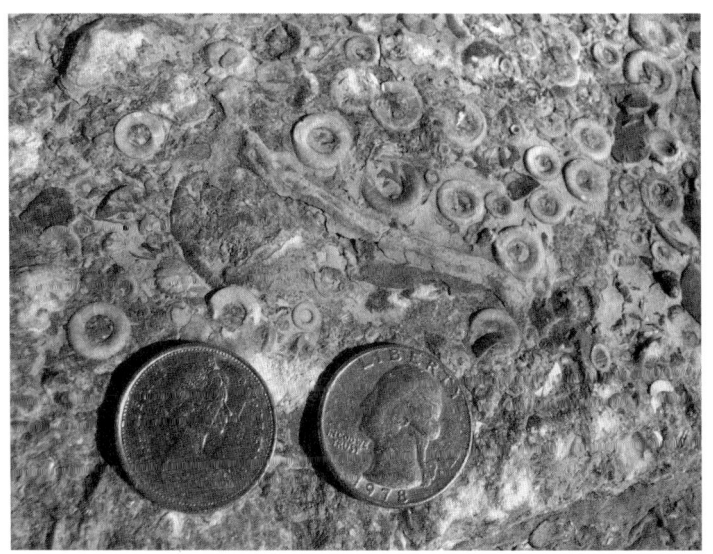

Crinoid fossils found in a rock "dump" one hundred yards before you cross the bridge onto Manitoulin Island

Crinoid stems

was discovered. When fish first evolved some 400 million years ago, they found that trilobites were good to eat. Just as modern bacteria evolve defenses against antibiotics, these trilobites started to evolve into forms not only able to defend themselves against fish (some trilobites evolved to become eurypterids that grew up to ten feet long) but also, in some cases, to even prey on fishes. Fish in turn responded by evolving defense mechanisms like armor plating. So began the battle between organisms with internal and external skeletons for supremacy on earth—a fight that continues to this day. (Fortunately for vertebrates like humans, the external skeletons of arthropods tend to

South shore of Manitoulin Island

impose size limitations on their owners.) Scorpions are eurypterids that left the sea, changed a little and learned to live on land where competition was less keen.

Anyone planning a visit to Manitoulin Island should consider purchasing *Manitoulin Rocks! Rocks, Fossils and Landforms of Manitoulin Island*, by Mario Coniglio, Paul Karrow, and Peter Russell (ISBN 978-0-9780993-0-5). This book gives detailed directions for a field trip that covers fifty collecting sites and areas of geological interest on Manitoulin Island.

Trans-Canada Highway to Blind River

Metamorphic Rock and Granite

This section of the route crosses rock similar to that between Sudbury and Espanola. It is 2.2 to 2.45 billion years old.

Points # 35–36 Blind River to Sault Ste. Marie

Metamorphic and Igneous Rock

Between Blind River and Sault Ste. Marie, three types of rock are present as bedrock and glacial debris: the Gowganda tillite, the Lorraine Formation (best known for an internal layer called puddingstone), and the Gordon Lake Formation (often called the banded cherty quartzite formation). These layers of rock differ in character from top to bottom, from east to west, and from north to south, but unusual and attractive stones can be cut from each.

Gowganda tillite is unsorted glacial debris, typically grayish black in color with interspersed orange granite pebbles. Some (if not most) of these granite pebbles appear to have been dropped after the initial glaciation event that brought the tillite when icebergs, floating in the sea, began to melt, dropping the pebbles. Below the

Gowganda tillite, the bedrock is covered with glaciation striations created 2.2 billion years ago. At this time, photosynthesizing algae and bacteria in the oceans produced so much oxygen that it began to interact with the atmosphere. The influx of oxygen resulted in the lowering of greenhouse gases, causing the earth's temperature to drop and creating glaciation across the planet—even apparently at the equator. During this period, the oceans froze to a depth of a half mile or more everywhere. Eventually, volcanism and its resulting carbon dioxide brought the big freeze (sometimes known as snowball earth) to an end.

Above the Gowganda tillite is a layer of puddingstone, so named for its resemblance to a pudding made by early French settlers. Puddingstone is composed of many types of quartz: white quartz sand from weathered granite, white vein quartz, red jasper, black flint, yellow chert, green quartz, and dark banded iron ore, interspersed with white kaolinite clay. All of these things, because they are virtually indestructible, are what weathering leaves behind. For more information on puddingstone, see page 70. Puddingstone can be cut into a variety of things, including beads, cabochons, lamp bases, and bookends.

Above the puddingstone lies Gordon Lake sediment consisting of mudstone, siltstone, chert, and quartzite. Ranging in color from red to yellow to green, Gordon

Lake sediment often features complex banding and vertical veins offset by miniature slump lines. The Gordon Lake sediment seems to have been deposited as soft sediment in a shallow lagoon. The slump lines within the rock were likely created before the sediment had hardened when earthquake activity caused one portion of the sediment to slip relative to the other. The result is a crazy, mixed-up pattern in the rock reminiscent of a Picasso painting. Gordon Lake sediment often polishes well.

Glacially transported Gowganda tillite, puddingstone, and Gordon Lake sediment can also be found on Manitoulin, Drummond, St. Joseph, and Sand islands. While much (if not most) of the loose material on these islands' shorelines has been picked through, there is plenty available in gravel pits around the area—do check with the owners first before entering one and be aware that there may be a nominal fee for collecting stones.

Just before the turn off to St. Joseph Island at S & S Creations near Bruce Mines, Stephanie Hitchell (phone: 705 785-2466) sells puddingstone and Gordon Lake deposit at her store on the Trans-Canada Highway—the address is 8418 Highway 17. Once on St. Joseph Island, there are a number of gravel pits, including one near the intersection of Hilton Road and Sideroad 10 and two on Hilton Road near Kentvale. Be sure to check with their owners before entering these pits.

Points # 37–39 Sault Ste. Marie to Drummond Island

Silurian Dolomite and Ordovician Shale

M-134 crosses Silurian dolomite similar to that found on Manitoulin Island. Like St. Joseph Island, Drummond Island is well known for its puddingstone. However, much of it has been picked up, and the local residents object to its removal from the island. A half mile past the intersection of M-134 and Shore and Townline roads, George Socia (phone: 906 493-5507) has a large gravel pit on the island and regularly finds

Collecting puddingstones at George Socia's pit

Puddingstone

Puddingstone at George Socia's

"Gone catching"

Even the most serious rock collector needs a pastime. Drummond Island is known for its fishing, and best to know this is a "catcher." I learned this phrase from my nine-year-old son one day. We were fishing from the same boat—I caught nothing; he caught two pike and two walleye. At day's end, he looked at me and said, "Dad, you catch nothing because you go fishing, but I go catching." To this day, when I ask, "Are you going fishing?" With a pole in hand, he turns, smiles, and says, "No. I'm going catching."

DANGER! LOOSE ROCKS CAN FALL AND WILL HURT YOU!

glacially transported Gowganda tillite and puddingstone, which he sells for nominal prices. Do not enter the quarry without permission.

On the north side of Drummond Island near Reynolds Bay and Poe Point, there is Ordovician shale that has been eroded to create a series of ledges covered with fossils—primarily coral, that has been replaced by quartz. The island's information center, located at Four Corners, can provide directions. The road to the fossil beds requires a four-wheel-drive vehicle—or, at the very least, a mental

Boy Scout Troop 35 saying on any outing—
Don't Get Dead!"

Over the last thirty years quarries, gravel pits, and the like have closed public rock collecting due to lawsuits brought against them. It only takes one person with a lack of common sense to close a gravel pit to public collecting. If you are wearing flip-flops, bathing suit, and carrying a plastic shovel you belong at the beach—*NOT at a gravel pit or quarry.* You may laugh, but while writing the *Lake Superior Rock Picker's Guide,* we encountered a family at the Ontario amethyst mines (with their razor sharp, freshly blasted rock) dressed in just such attire. Always use common sense. *Never* go near any overhang of loose rocks for any reason. Respect the owner's equipment and instructions. Wear heavy boots, jeans, and gloves when collecting. Keep in mind gravel pits are in operation to move and sell rock by the ton—it is a privilege to be invited in for personal collecting. Treat it as a privilege, and if you are there for just a few rocks, then compensate for the owner's time, not just the weight of the rocks. I would like to believe years after this book comes to market I still can spend an afternoon in this gravel pit and not have to keep it a secret.

Sunrise perch fishing on Drummond Island

attitude that lies somewhere between reckless and foolhardy. The residents of the island request that these fossils be left in place for future generations to see and enjoy.

From Drummond Island, a return to the Big Mac Bridge will bring us to where this trip started.

What Types of Rocks Are Found on Lake Huron?

Basalt

Basalt is the hard black or dark green rock often found on beaches. Basalt typically lacks character, though occasionally veins of quartz run through it—and these specimens, representations of nature's artwork, are often worth collecting. Because of its hardness, basalt was prized by local Native Americans for hammer stones in making arrowheads and used to grind corn and herbs. For farmers, however, basalt is a nuisance because of its weight to move.

Chain coral

As its name suggests, this stone features many white chains interlocking a tan matrix. The white lines are the actual coral, which can be extracted using the muriatic acid bath discussed on pages 23–24. Chain coral is most common in the eastern Upper Peninsula and on Drummond Island, however, it can also be found around Lake Michigan. Even on a really good day, you will likely find only a half dozen specimens, typically no bigger than two to three inches. Photos of some excellently preserved chain coral appear in this book's color section.

Chert

Chert is microcrystalline quartz and comes in a variety of colors. Chert can be one solid color or banded, and it is typically opaque. Like agate, chert frequently features conchoidal fractures—curved breakage surfaces often resembling the rippled arc of a mussel shell—and so the two rocks can be easily confused. They can be distinguished in a number of ways, though. First, chert is opaque. Second, though less dependably, chert is typically tan-cream in color and, on rare occasion, a tan-red.

Cladopora

A branching form of coral during Silurian and Devonian times, cladopora was not unlike the bleached white staghorn coral you occasionally see at pet stores. Fossilized after being buried in limey mud, cladopora often occurs as a gray-white coral in a jet black stone saturated with crude oil, which gives the stone its color. Since cladopora is usually found on the beach rather than in bedrock, determining its age and place of origin can be difficult. Specimens are usually from Silurian bedrock of the Upper Peninsula or the Devonian bedrock of the Lower Peninsula.

Crinoids

Crinoids were marine relatives of sea stars that can be best understood by studying the three pictures in the color photo section. The stems of these organisms were formed by many "disks" stacked on top of each other. When the organism died, these disks separated, with the top portion going first. Because of this, the tops of crinoids, which look something like an octopus, are very rare. The fossilized disk portions are less rare and are normally found on beaches in round rock form. See the color photo section for examples of a crinoid stem, top, and disk. The crinoids samples collected near Manitoulin Island provide amazing insight into how the stone on the beach formed.

Years after the release of our first book, *Lake Michigan Rock Picker's Guide,* people still come to us with fossilized crinoids, claiming they have found "a petrified eyeball from a reptile." One visitor even thought he had discovered a petrified monkey. Even after being shown what the rock really is, these people look at us like we have no idea what we're talking about and do not understand their find. We usually smile and agree— "Maybe you did find a petrified eyeball." Thank goodness for the crinoids. They keep people guessing.

Dolomite

Dolomite looks like a plain white rock, and outcroppings of it can be seen when crossing the Mackinac Bridge into the Upper Peninsula just beyond the rest area. Other places dolomite is common include the northern shores of Drummond Island and the Bruce Peninsula, both of which are home to a large amount of dolomite filled with holes—our best guess is that these are places where lichen has "eaten" into the rock enough to allow water to accumulate and dissolve the material. The Bruce Peninsula's east side is also primarily dolomite. When dolomite underlies a body of water, the water appears an intense Caribbean blue when viewed from above. See the color photo section for a photo taken looking off a pier at dolomite in fifteen feet of water as well as one of a pool inside a dolomite cave.

Favosite fossils (Charlevoix stone)

This fossil is often mistakenly thought to be a miniature Petoskey stone or one that did not form completely. Favosites are actually formed by a different coral than the Petoskey. When cut and polished perpendicular to their eye chambers (which are round and interlocking like in a Petoskey stone, but smaller), favosites can take on woodlike grain (see the color photo section).

Feldspar

Feldspar is typically pink, but it also comes in a variety of other colors, including yellow. It is normally a single color. Feldspar looks very similar to quartz but can be distinguished by the sheen it puts off in the light. This sheen is seen better when the rock is dry and best when the day is bright and sunny. Held at an angle, the stone will reflect light almost like a mirror—this is because feldspar has a defined cleavage plane. Both feldspar and quartz can be found in most of the granite that formed in the Canadian Shield and was carried to the Great Lakes by the glaciers. The result is quartz and feldspar pebbles throughout the region—treasures to put in our pockets.

Gowganda tillite

Often found on the northeast shore of Lake Michigan, Gowganda tillite is of the same age and area as puddingstone. Gowganda tillite features round, attractive granite pebbles embedded in a dark gray matrix. See page 52 for more information.

Granite

When you find a colorful rock with a speckled pattern, it is most likely granite. Granite's color is derived from the minerals within it and typically includes pink (feldspar), white (quartz), and black biotite (mica). Other colors will vary from reds, greens, tans, and creams. Granite does not make up Michigan's local bedrock. Rather, the granite now scattered across the Great Lakes region was once part of the Canadian Shield. This granite was broken down by weathering and transported by glacial action into Michigan. Today, hundreds of tons of granite are used for construction and landscaping each year.

Honeycomb coral

This coral looks like the honeycomb of a beehive. For years, I only found this fossil replaced by quartz and came to believe it would always have a yellowish color indicative of that process—until doing research on this book, that is. On the north shore of Drummond Island, Fossil Point, I came across a fossil I was not familiar with. It looked something like a Petoskey, but it was not. Upon further study I came to the conclusion it was honeycomb coral that had been calcified—though, it's possible the fossil was another variety honeycomb coral. See the color photo section for photos of the two types of fossils.

Most fossils found in the Great Lakes will be calcified or replaced by quartz.

Calcified—the coral's porous structure was filled by the mineral calcite, typical of most Petoskey stones. Calcite is soft, and when this type of fossilization takes place, the stone can be scratched with a knife blade. The original coral structure was also calcite.

Quartz replaced—the coral's porous structure was filled by the mineral quartz. If you ever found a Petoskey stone where the centers of the eyes are raised and look like a bunch of "miniature mountains," you have found a quartz-filled Petoskey. The hexagon coral original structure is eroded deeper into the stone leaving raised bumps of quartz.

Horn corals

Full specimens of horn coral are easily identified by their horn shape—large at one end tapered to thin at the other. Horn coral fragments are often more difficult to recognize. End fragments can be identified by their large eye, which look similar to a single Petoskey stone "eye." Fragments from the sidewall of this coral can be deceiving unless you visualize the shape and top view of a full fossil. Sidewall fragments will have one of two characteristics, depending on which part of the coral the fragment came from and how large the coral was. Some fragments will have parallel lines, indicating either that the fragment came from higher up on the coral or was from a particularly large coral. Other fragments will have lines that angle toward a single point, indicating either that the fragment came from the tip of the coral or was from a smaller organism. Identification of horn coral fragments can be especially difficult when their sidewall lines become exposed through siltstone or shale. Many people have come to us claiming to have discovered a fossilized bone, only to find out it was the side view of a horn coral. Studying the pictures in the color photo section—in particular, the shape of the coral fossils, where the lines start and end, and what the tops look like—can help when it comes to recognizing this fossil.

Jasper

Jasper is quartz with enough iron to give it an attractive red or yellow color. It can be cut and polished to produce an attractive, inexpensive gemstone. Around two billion years old, most jasper comes from the iron ore deposits around Marquette. Though more common on the west shore of the Lake Michigan, jasper can also be found in Lake Huron. Sometimes it is found banded with iron ore or other types of quartz.

Kettle stones

Kettle stones are also referred to as concretions. They are balls of limey mud, basketball- to boulder-sized. Kettle stones are often found within the Antrim Shale. See the discussion of Kettle Point on pages 37–39.

Petoskey stones—Michigan's state stone

Petoskey stones are a fossilized coral that has an "eye" like pattern similar to today's brain coral. Petoskey stones will appear whitish-gray when dry and darker gray when wet. They are Michigan's state stone. Note: Michigan does have a state gem—greenstone. For more information about Petoskey stones, including detailed locations of where to find them, see *The Complete Guide to Petoskey Stones* (ISBN 978-0-472-03028-6).

Pipe organ coral

Pipe organ corals look very similar to horn corals. In fact, without a large piece to examine or a horn coral specimen with the tip worn, it is virtually impossible to tell the two apart. Whereas horn corals grew as individual specimens (almost like single carrots with their smaller ends attached to the seafloor), pipe organ coral grew as many neighboring tubes—much like its namesake pipe organ.

Puddingstones

Puddingstones are featured on the front cover of this book. The pebbles in puddingstone are the remains of weathering that occurred around 2 billion years ago. Because puddingstone is composed mostly of quartz, we know this weathering process occurred in a humid, probably tropical climate that helped dissolve and remove nonquartz minerals. Metamorphism later fused the remaining quartz together. The body of puddingstone will be white intermixed with pebbles ranging in color from red to black to tan to green. Puddingstone can be found on the northeastern shore of Lake Michigan, but it is much more common on the northeast side of the state near Lake Huron and in particular in the vicinity of Elliot Lake, Ontario. Gravel pits near Elliot Lake as well as on St. Joseph and Drummond islands are good spots to find puddingstone, though the rock can also be found in Michigan's Lower Peninsula where some of the most recent glacial activity transported it. Boulder-sized puddingstone can occasionally be found in farmers' fields near Clare, Michigan—if you know a farmer in this area, ask permission to look though the windrow of rocks they may have accumulated.

Quartz

Everyone loves to find a round white quartz rock on the beach, perfectly smooth and transparent. Pure quartz comes in a variety of colors, but a cream to a yellow is the most commonly found. Other colors include pure snow white, burgundy, and pink (note, however, that feldspar is also pink, but less transparent than quartz). The body of quartz is usually a single color.

A large percentage of the earth's surface is covered with quartz, and it is a primary ingredient in many other stones such as granite, agate, chert, and feldspar. Sand is composed mostly of quartz, and glass is as well—from skyscraper windows to bottles to eyeglasses to the mirror you view yourself in. It is an important mineral to our way of life.

Sandstone

Just as it sounds, sandstone is sand that has been pressed together. It comes in a variety of colors. When examined closely, the stone's surface resembles a bunch of sand grains stuck together. Also when the stone is dry, put a couple droplets of water on it and they will absorb into the surface almost instantaneously.

Stromatoporoid

Found around both Lake Michigan and Lake Huron, some stromatoporoids are fossilized sponges that are banded in layers; others are fossilized algae. Lucky rock pickers will sometimes find a "twofer" of stromatoporoids attached to corals such as Petoskey or favosite fossils—two fossils in one (see photo in the color photo section). A number of stromatoporoids have been found imbedded in the bedrock on Drummond Island.

Syringopora

We sometimes refer to Syringogpora, another type of fossilized coral, as tube fossils. See the color photo section to view the parallel tubes from which this nickname is derived. These tubes are attached at the top to hold the whole coral together.

Trilobite

Flat, recently split stone surfaces are good places to find trilobites, meaning quarries where rock is broken are some of the best locations to look. Unfortunately, permission to enter such quarries is seldom given. The most commonly found

Devonian trilobite is *Phacops rana*. The most commonly found Silurian trilobite is calamene, Wisconsin's state fossil. Dalmanites are also common in Silurian rock.

Unakite

Unakite is an orange or pinkish granite containing intrusions (sometimes streaks) of light green epidote. New England states mine unakite as an inexpensive gemstone. The rock is also found on both sides of Lake Huron, and some of this is of the highest quality. Properly cut and polished, it can create some very unique jewelry pieces.

The Passion of Rock Collecting

There are two kinds of people: those who love rocks and those who couldn't care less about them. If you have bought and/or are reading this rock collecting book, you belong to the first—and correct!—category.

The passion of rock collecting is more than the hobby itself. Rock collecting goes to the heart of human compassion by involving an inner connection with nature that is uplifting, spiritual, rewarding, challenging, full of discovery, and tied with a common bond of companionship. However, very few people think of rock collecting in such a manner.

Consciously or unconsciously, when rock collecting, we connect with our surroundings: a sunset, the sounds of waves and gulls, fresh smells of the Great Lakes, or even just a smile from another beach walker. Somehow, these moments become part of us, and the stones we pick up become physical ties to them. Rock hounding memories can be made on an individual basis or shared with all generations—on a romantic walk or a family day, while watching the sun rise or set, even on those days when you just decide to take a walk alone. In any case, we come back with a rock—a memory. It may be why people cherish their rock collections with such passion.

The hobby can be very rewarding and lead to the discovery of unique rocks the likes of which no one else has. These are the special rocks we have vivid memories of finding; they are the coolest pieces of our collections and, naturally, the ones we pull out first to show others. Deep down, there's the little child inside of us gloating, "Na, Na, Nanna—I have the coolest one!" Kind of like going to the ice cream store—everyone else gets the standard flavors, but you venture out and get the unknown. Then everyone else wants a taste of yours.

For the serious rock collector, the hunt for ever more variety can be a major attraction. The Internet has contributed a large part to this. We are always looking for that rare unique specimen to add to our collection. For some, the adventure of finding new spots that no one else knows about to expand our collections is another lure. The challenges rock collectors face are many—in particular, once off the beaten path, carrying the bounty back from that place! Even more difficult can be convincing that other kind of person—those who passed up this book—that YES, the car will handle this much weight, and NO, we can't put any rocks back.

Discovery is such a large part of rock collecting. Volumes of books could be written on just this. Over the past thirty-seven years of collecting it may be best summed up with a simple picture—the caterpillar.

Without this passion I would have missed out on many experiences with nature like this rare white caterpiller.

Companionship and compassion go hand in hand. Just like any hobby—whether it be hiking, kayaking, or hunting—it is ultimately sharing with others that makes rock collecting so rewarding. As a member of our local rock club (www.tcrockhounds.com), part of the Midwest Federation of Mineralogical and Geological Societies, I have made more lifetime bonds than through any other club. Those who share this passion always have a good story to tell, are willing to share a campfire, and generally enjoy life. I highly encourage you to join a local club in your area. If one doesn't exist, share the passion and start one.